Truck travel

Trucks carry all kinds of things from one place to another.

The things a truck carries are called its load.

Trucks and trailers

Some trucks come in two parts. The trailer is where the load is kept and the front part is known as a 'tractor'.

The place where the driver sits is called the cab.

Wires and tubes carry electricity and air to the trailer. These make the back lights and brakes work.

The trailer rests on two landing legs.

The tractor backs to meet the trailer.

They join together and drive away.

When trailer trucks reach a bend, the tractor turns first, then the trailer follows.

A tractor can join up with different shapes of trailers.

5

Truck bodies

Not all trucks have two parts. On many trucks the trailer is fixed to the cab.

This truck is taking fresh bananas to market.

Some very small trucks only have three wheels.

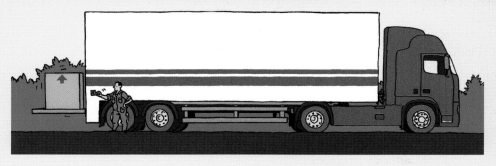

Box body trucks have hard sides and open up at the back.

Curtain-sider trucks have sides which open like a big curtain.

On flatbed trucks, the load lies flat on the trailer and is tied down with rope.

Loading up

Lots of trucks collect their loads from huge buildings called warehouses.

A forklift truck picks up a crate on a pallet.

It takes it outside and lifts it up onto a truck.

The crates are stacked inside the truck.

Some loads, such as racehorses, can walk onto their trucks.

This truck has its own crane. The driver is using it to load up.

On the road

Often trucks have to take their load to somewhere far away.

The journey may take several days.

Many countries make drivers take a break during the day so they don't get too tired.

Truck drivers take breaks at truck stops.

On long journeys they can rest, eat and sleep in their trucks.

Inside the cab there is room to relax.

A bed folds down from the wall.

Across the sea

Trucks may have to take their loads across the sea on a ferry.

Trucks arrive at a port. They drive up a ramp, onto a ferry.

The ferry closes its back door and sets sail across the sea.

When it reaches land, the front of the ferry opens and the trucks drive off.

Some loads are lifted onto a ship, leaving the truck behind.

The ship crosses the sea and the load is put on another truck.

The load travels inside a box called a container. Cranes lift the containers on and off the ship.

Container crane

Containers

Tanker trucks

Tanker trucks carry liquids or gases in big tanks on their trailers.

Milk tankers collect milk from farms. The milk goes through a pipe into the tank.

Cows are milked twice a day. The tanker collects the milk on the same day.

Fuel tankers take
fuel to petrol stations.

At the petrol
station, pipes are
fixed to the tanker.

The fuel goes from
the tanker into big
tanks under the ground.

Fuel
tank

Fuel
tank

15

Dumpers

Dump trucks are huge trucks that carry sand, earth and chunks of rock.

The driver has to climb up some steps to reach the cab.

A big digger fills
the truck with
scoops of earth.

The truck takes the
earth away, then
dumps it out.

Some dump
trucks have
wheels taller
than two
tall men.

Fire engines

Fire engines are trucks that bring ladders and water to places where there's a fire.

The firefighters open up the side to reach their equipment.

They unwind hoses and fix them to the truck's water tank.

If the water tank runs out, they use water from pipes under the ground.

Ladders stretch up from the back of the trucks and firefighters spray water on the fire.

Some fire engines have platforms that reach up to rescue people.

Heavy loads

Trucks that carry big, heavy loads have many wheels or move on tracks.

This transporter truck is carrying a space shuttle. Can you see the truck cab?

The transporter takes the shuttle into a warehouse.

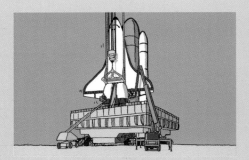

Cranes help lift the shuttle onto a crawler truck.

Space shuttle

The crawler has tracks instead of wheels. It carries the shuttle to its launch pad.

Track

The shuttle crawler travels even slower than a person walking.

Dirty work

Refuse collectors collect rubbish and carry it away in rubbish trucks.

A rubbish bin is hooked onto the truck. It is lifted up and the rubbish is tipped out.

A big metal plate squashes down the rubbish to make more room.

To empty the truck, the end lifts up and a metal plate pushes the rubbish out.

A bigger truck takes the rubbish to a place where it can be burned or buried.

Some rubbish can be used again. This tipper truck is delivering plastic bags to a recycling point.

Hot and cold

Around the world, trucks are shaped differently to suit the jobs they do.

Road trains are big trucks with several trailers.

They travel long distances on very straight roads. Some drive right across deserts.

Road trains meet very little traffic so they can travel quickly.

In snowy mountains,
trucks are used to flatten
the snow on the ski slopes.

They have tracks instead of wheels to stop
them slipping on the snow.

The front of the
truck scoops snow
out of the way.

At the back there
are brushes to
smooth the snow.

Car transporters

Car transporters carry cars to garages.
Follow the numbers to see how they load up.

Deck

1. A car reverses onto a deck and is tipped up.

2. Two cars follow, then that deck is raised.

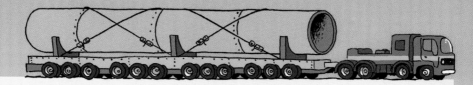

Some trucks have more than 50 wheels.

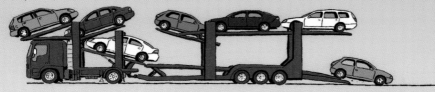

3. Three cars drive onto a deck above the cab.

4. Six more cars fit onto other decks below.

Truck sports

Some trucks don't carry loads. Instead they take part in truck sports.

These trucks are having a race. They drive around a track at top speed.

Some very fast trucks have jet engines, just like planes.

Once a year there is a truck race that goes across the Sahara desert and takes 21 days.

Monster trucks take part in jumping competitions.

| The monster truck speeds up a ramp. | It jumps up and over a big object. | Then it lands with a bump on the ground. |

Glossary of truck words

Here are some of the words in this book you might not know. This page tells you what they mean.

 load - the things carried by a truck.

 cab - the front part of a truck where the truck driver sits.

 trailer - a load carrier on wheels that is pulled by a truck.

 pallet - a big tray used in warehouses. Forklift trucks lift up crates on pallets.

 truck stop - like a car park, but for trucks. Drivers can stay the night here.

 ferry - a boat which takes people, trucks and cars across the sea.

 recycling - making new objects from old objects that are collected by trucks.

Web sites to visit

If you have a computer, you can find out more about trucks on the Internet. On the Usborne Quicklinks Web site there are links to four fun Web sites.

Web site 1 - Make different trucks with the three cards on your screen.

Web site 2 - Find out more about dump trucks and building sites.

Web site 3 - See photos of trucks from around the world.

Web site 4 - Learn what each part of a fire engine does.

To visit these Web sites, go to **www.usborne-quicklinks.com** and type the keywords "beginners trucks". Then click on the link for the Web site you want to visit. Before you use the Internet, look at the safety guidelines inside the back cover of this book and ask an adult to read them with you.

Index

Acknowledgements

Managing editor: Fiona Watt, Managing designer: Mary Cartwright
Photographic manipulation by Emma Julings and John Russell

Photo credits

The publishers are grateful to the following for permission to reproduce material:
© **Alvey & Towers** Cover, 1, 5, 28, © **Bill Noonan, Boston Fire Department** 19,
© **Corbis** (Kevin R. Morris) 6, (Joseph Sohm; ChromoSohm Inc.) 9, (Ted Spiegel) 11,
(Richard Hamilton Smith) 16-17, (Richard T. Nowitz) 23, (Christine Osborne) 24,
© **The Dairy Council** 14, © **Digital Vision** 4, 10, 12-13, 16-17, 23, 24, © **ECM (Vehicle
Delivery Service) Ltd** 26-27, © **Kässbohrer Geländefahrzeug AG (PistenBully)** 25,
© **Malcolm Birks** 31, © **NASA** 20, 21, © **Nissan/dppi** 29, © **Volvo Truck Limited** 2-3, 15

With thanks to

Henry Brook, Chris Hodge Trucks (www.chrishodgetrucks.co.uk),
Bill Noonan, Steven Askew, Wolfgang Lutz and The Dairy Council